Top 50 Yummy Green Bean Recipes

(Top 50 Yummy Green Bean Recipes - Volume 1)

Pauline Harmon

Content

50 Awesome Green Bean Recipes

***

1. 30 Minute Almond Chicken By Minute® Rice

Serving: 4 | Prep: | Ready in:

Ingredients

- 8 boneless, skinless chicken thighs
- 1/4 cup Italian dressing
- 1 1/2 cups chicken broth
- 2 cups green beans, trimmed, halved
- 1 cup Minute® White Rice, uncooked
- 1/4 cup almonds, sliced

Direction

- In a sealable plastic bag, toss chicken with dressing. Place a large nonstick skillet on medium-high heat; put in the chicken with dressing; cook till browned, or 4 minutes per side.
- Mix in broth; allow to boil. Simmer with a cover for 10 minutes. Put in beans; cook till the chicken is heated through (170°F), or for 5 minutes.
- Take the chicken out of the skillet. Put in almonds and rice. Take away from the heat. Allow to stand with a cover for 5 minutes. Serve chicken over the prepared rice mixture.

Nutrition Information

- Calories: 682 calories;
- Total Fat: 42.2
- Sodium: 782
- Total Carbohydrate: 29.4
- Cholesterol: 193
- Protein: 44.5

2. Air Fryer Green Beans With Spicy Dipping Sauce

Serving: 4 | Prep: 15mins | Ready in:

Ingredients

- 1 cup beer
- 1 cup all-purpose flour
- 2 teaspoons salt
- 1/2 teaspoon ground black pepper
- 1 (12 ounce) package fresh green beans, trimmed
- parchment paper cut to the size of the air fryer basket
- Dipping Sauce:
- 1 cup ranch dressing
- 2 teaspoons sriracha sauce
- 1 teaspoon prepared horseradish, or to taste

Direction

- Combine pepper, salt, flour and beer in a bowl. Coat the beans with batter in the small batches and shake off the excess.
- Preheat the air fryer to 200 degrees C (400 degrees F) following the direction of manufacturers.
- Line parchment paper on bottom of air fryer basket. Add one single layer of battered beans into the air fryer. Cook for 8-10 minutes till turning golden brown and crisp on outside. Repeat the process with all the rest of the battered beans.
- In a bowl, combine horseradish, sriracha sauce and ranch dressing. Serve along with green beans.

Nutrition Information

- Calories: 466 calories;
- Total Carbohydrate: 35.4
- Cholesterol: 16
- Total Fat: 31.6
- Protein: 5.9
- Sodium: 1863

3. Airport Bob's Green Beans

Serving: 6 | Prep: 10mins | Ready in:

Ingredients

- 6 thick slices bacon, cut into 1 inch pieces
- 1 (16 ounce) package frozen cut green beans
- 1/4 cup butter
- 1/4 cup packed brown sugar

Direction

- In a large skillet, fry the bacon on medium heat for 9 minutes until it's done yet not really crisp. Drain grease and put in brown sugar and butter. Stir and cook on medium heat until the sugar dissolves; take away from the heat, then put aside.
- Fill a pot with roughly an inch of water and put in green beans. Boil, then put a cover and steam on medium heat for 5 minutes until cook fully. Drain the water and stir in the bacon mixture and sugar. Serve right away.

Nutrition Information

- Calories: 195 calories;
- Protein: 5.7
- Total Fat: 12.9
- Sodium: 347
- Total Carbohydrate: 14
- Cholesterol: 34

4. Authentic Paella Valenciana

Serving: 8 | Prep: 30mins | Ready in:

Ingredients

- 1 tablespoon olive oil
- 1/2 (4 pound) whole chicken, cut into 6 pieces
- 1/2 (2 pound) rabbit, cleaned and cut into pieces
- 1 head garlic, cloves separated and peeled
- 1 tomato, finely chopped
- 1 (15.5 ounce) can butter beans
- 1/2 (10 ounce) package frozen green peas
- 1/2 (10 ounce) package frozen green beans
- salt to taste
- 1 teaspoon mild paprika, or to taste
- 1 pinch saffron threads
- dried thyme to taste (optional)
- dried rosemary to taste (optional)
- 4 cups uncooked white rice, or as needed

Direction

- Heat paella pan on medium high heat; coat in olive oil. Add garlic, rabbit and chicken; mix and cook till browned nicely. Move browned meat to sides of pan; add green beans, peas, butter beans and tomato. Season with paprika; stir well.
- Pour water in paella pan until nearly to the top; measure water out while adding. This is to help you know how much rice to put in because paella pans can be of different sizes. Boil. Simmer to make nice broth for 1 hour.
- Season with enough saffron to create nice yellow color and generous amount of salt. Season if desired with rosemary and thyme. The goal is to achieve a flavorful broth to soak into the rice for it to be delicious. Mix in 1/2 as much rice as the amount of water in pan. Cover; lower heat to low; simmer for20 minutes till all liquid is absorbed.

Nutrition Information

- Calories: 783 calories;

- Total Fat: 31.3
- Sodium: 328
- Total Carbohydrate: 87.3
- Cholesterol: 82
- Protein: 34.2

5. Bacon Wrapped Green Beans

Serving: 8 | Prep: 15mins | Ready in:

Ingredients

- 1 (12 ounce) package bacon, strips cut in half
- 1 (16 ounce) package frozen cut green beans
- 2 tablespoons brown sugar
- salt and pepper to taste

Direction

- Apply grease to a casserole dish and preheat the oven to 175°C or 350°F.
- Prepare the green beans and bacon and casserole dish in a little assembly line. Take half a strip of bacon and fill it with a small amount of green beans (6 to 7) onto the strip of bacon and roll up into a bundle. Place the bundle into the casserole dish with the seam side down.
- Repeat with remaining bacon strips and green beans. You can pack these pretty tight in the pan, just know that if the bacon is touching another bundle they take some prying to get apart.
- Drizzle the top with salt, pepper and brown sugar.
- Let it bake in the preheated oven for about 20 minutes until it becomes brown and heated through.

Nutrition Information

- Calories: 226 calories;
- Total Fat: 19.2
- Sodium: 355

- Total Carbohydrate: 7.2
- Cholesterol: 29
- Protein: 5.7

6. Cauliflower Bean Casserole

Serving: 10 | Prep: 15mins | Ready in:

Ingredients

- 1 head cauliflower, cut into florets
- 1 (9 ounce) package frozen cut green beans
- 1 (12 ounce) package bacon, cut in half crosswise
- 1 small onion, chopped
- 1/2 cup butter, softened
- 1 cup mayonnaise
- 1 cup grated mozzarella cheese

Direction

- Preheat the oven to 150 degrees C (300 degrees F).
- Boil a large pot of lightly salted water; cook cauliflower about 10 minutes, or until softened but still firm to the bite. Add green beans; cook for another 5 minutes, or until tender. Drain.
- In a large skillet, place bacon and cook over medium-high heat for about 10 minutes, occasionally turning, or until browned evenly. Drain the bacon slices on paper towels, saving the bacon grease in the skillet.
- Over medium heat, cook and stir onion with bacon grease in the skillet for about 10 minutes, or until soft and lightly browned.
- Mix onion, bacon, green beans, and cauliflower together in a casserole dish.
- In a bowl, stir together mayonnaise and butter; pour over the cauliflower mixture. Then stir to coat; put mozzarella cheese on top.
- Bake in the preheated oven for 20 minutes, or until the cheese is melted and bubbling.

Nutrition Information

- Calories: 354 calories;
- Total Fat: 33.2
- Sodium: 537
- Total Carbohydrate: 6.5
- Cholesterol: 52
- Protein: 8.7

7. Chickpea Maltagliati E Fagioli

Serving: 4 | Prep: 30mins | Ready in:

Ingredients

- 1 cup dried cranberry beans
- 2 sprigs fresh sage
- 1 sprig fresh rosemary
- 1 bay leaf
- kitchen twine
- 4 ounces chickpea lasagna sheets
- 2 tablespoons olive oil
- 1/2 cup diced onion
- 1/2 cup diced carrots
- 1/2 cup diced red bell pepper
- 20 fresh green beans, cut into 1-inch pieces
- 10 cherry tomatoes, quartered
- 1 clove garlic, minced
- 1 bird's eye chile, minced (optional)
- 4 cups water
- 1 cube vegetable bouillon
- salt and ground black pepper to taste
- 2 cups boiling water (optional)
- 4 teaspoons extra-virgin olive oil
-

Direction

- Immerse the beans for 8 hours to overnight in the water.
- Allow the beans to drain and quickly rinse it under cold water.
- Tie bay leaf, sage, and rosemary with kitchen twine, and then set aside for a while. Crack the lasagna sheets into uneven parts but relatively in same size.

- Preheat the stovetop pressure cooker over medium-high heat. Stir in onion, red bell pepper, 2 tbsp. of oil, and carrots. Cook until the onion is translucent. Mix in drained beans, cherry tomatoes, herb bundle, chile pepper, garlic, and green beans. Stir to make sure the beans are equally distributed. Add bouillon cube and 4 cups of water. Lock the lid tightly and bring to pressure. After hearing the first whistle, start its cooking time for 8 minutes.
- Remove it from heat and let the pressure release naturally according to manufacturer's directions. Unlock and remove the herb bundle. Flavor the stew with pepper and salt. Let it boil. Add the pasta pieces, few at a time, while stirring it constantly to avoid sticking to each other.
- When the stew becomes thick, pour small amount of boiling water a little at a time. Stir for 8 minutes until the pasta is soft and firm to bite. Distribute the stew into 4 bowls and top each with 1 tsp. of extra-virgin olive oil.

Nutrition Information

- Calories: 398 calories;
- Protein: 18
- Sodium: 85
- Total Carbohydrate: 54
- Cholesterol: 0
- Total Fat: 13.5

8. Cold Green Bean Salad

Serving: 8 | Prep: 10mins | Ready in:

Ingredients

- 2 (15 ounce) cans green beans, drained
- 1 red onion, sliced in rings
- 1 (16 ounce) bottle Italian-style salad dressing

Direction

- In a serving dish, add beans, then toss together with salad dressing and onions. Use plastic wrap to cover and refrigerate about 1 hour.

Nutrition Information

- Calories: 184 calories;
- Total Fat: 15.7
- Sodium: 1213
- Total Carbohydrate: 10.6
- Cholesterol: 0
- Protein: 1.2

9. Colorful Four Bean Salad

Serving: 12 | Prep: 20mins | Ready in:

Ingredients

- 1 cup white sugar
- 1 cup white vinegar
- 1 tablespoon vegetable oil
- 6 stalks celery, chopped
- 1 green bell pepper, seeded and chopped
- 1 medium red onion, chopped
- 1 (4 ounce) jar pimento peppers, drained and chopped
- 1 (14 ounce) can cut green beans
- 1 (14.5 ounce) can yellow wax beans
- 1 (15 ounce) can lima beans
- 1 (15 ounce) can dark red kidney beans

Direction

- Whisk together vegetable oil, vinegar and white sugar in a big bowl, then stir in pimentos, red onion, green pepper and celery. In a colander, add kidney beans, lima beans, wax beans and green beans then rinse with running cold water. Allow to drain for a couple of minutes, then mix into the bowl with the rest of the salad. Keep in a big jar in the fridge and turn sometimes or shake, for 1 day to marinate. Simply stir the salad for every few

hours in case you don't have a sealed container. This can be kept for a week, but will be gone soon.

Nutrition Information

- Calories: 154 calories;
- Total Fat: 1.4
- Sodium: 416
- Total Carbohydrate: 31.9
- Cholesterol: 0
- Protein: 4.6

10. Creamy String Bean Soup

Serving: 6 | Prep: | Ready in:

Ingredients

- 1 (15 ounce) can cut green beans
- 4 potatoes, diced
- 2 tablespoons distilled white vinegar
- 1 clove garlic
- 1 cup sour cream
- salt and pepper to taste
- 2 tablespoons all-purpose flour
- 1/4 cup water
- 1 yellow onion, chopped

Direction

- Cook the potatoes in the salted water. Once halfway cooked, put in the pepper, vinegar and beans, garlic (spear on the toothpick in order to be easy to find). Put in the onion. Let it simmer till the potatoes are done. Take out the garlic glove.
- Mix a quarter cup of the water and flour and form a smooth paste. Thicken the soup using flour paste.
- Take out of the heat. Gradually whisk in the sour cream. Don't cook more. Whisk in cooked and diced Mettwurst or other German sausage just prior to serving.

Nutrition Information

- Calories: 221 calories;
- Sodium: 228
- Total Carbohydrate: 32.6
- Cholesterol: 17
- Protein: 5.2
- Total Fat: 8.2

11. Divine Chicken With Green Beans

Serving: 4 | Prep: 5mins | Ready in:

Ingredients

- 2 tablespoons olive oil
- 1 pound skinless, boneless chicken breast halves - diced
- 1 tablespoon minced garlic, or to taste
- 1/4 cup thinly sliced onion
- 12 ounces fresh or frozen green beans
- 1/4 cup grated Parmesan cheese
- 3 tablespoons heavy cream

Direction

- In a large skillet, heat the oil over medium-high heat. Put in chicken and cook until it is browned. Add onion and garlic, turn down the heat to medium. Stir and cook until they are just fragrant. Stir in green beans, put on a cover and cook for 5 minutes or more to reach the desired doneness.
- Remove the cover and stir in cheese and cream until everything is just covered. Take away from the heat and serve.

Nutrition Information

- Calories: 278 calories;
- Cholesterol: 86
- Protein: 30.2

- Total Fat: 13.8
- Sodium: 161
- Total Carbohydrate: 8.3

12. Fresh Green Bean And Mushroom Casserole

Serving: 6 | Prep: 25mins | Ready in:

Ingredients

- 1 1/2 pounds fresh green beans, trimmed and cut into bite-size pieces
- 2 tablespoons butter or margarine
- 3 tablespoons all-purpose flour
- 1 tablespoon ranch dressing mix
- 1/4 teaspoon ground white pepper
- 1 1/2 cups fat-free milk
- cooking spray
- 1 cup chopped onion
- 2 cloves garlic, minced
- 1 1/2 cups sliced fresh mushrooms
- 1 cup panko bread crumbs

Direction

- Preheat the oven to 190 degrees C (375 degrees F).
- Boil the big pot of the slightly salted water. Put in the green beans and cook, while uncovering, for 10-15 minutes till becoming soft but still firm to bite. Drain.
- Melt the butter on medium heat in a sauce pan; stir the white pepper, ranch dressing mix and flour into the butter till forming a paste-liked consistency. Add the milk to the butter mixture; cook, stir continuously, for 5-10 minutes till the sauce becomes thickened and bubbling.
- Use the cooking spray to spray one non-stick skillet and position on medium heat. Cook and whisk the garlic and onion in the hot skillet for roughly 2 minutes till becoming tender slightly. Move half of the onion mixture into a plate and bring the skillet back to the heat.

- Whisk the mushrooms into the skillet with the rest of the onion mixture; cook and whisk for roughly 5 minutes or till the mushrooms soften.
- Whisk together the sauce, green beans and mushroom mixture in a 1.5-qt. casserole dish. Whisk together the bread crumbs and the reserved onion mixture in a bowl; drizzle on the green bean mixture.
- Bake in preheated oven for 25-30 minutes till becoming hot and bubbly.

Nutrition Information

- Calories: 169 calories;
- Total Fat: 4.8
- Sodium: 232
- Total Carbohydrate: 30.7
- Cholesterol: 11
- Protein: 7.4

13. Georgian Green Beans

Serving: 10 | Prep: 15mins | Ready in:

Ingredients

- 2 pounds fresh green beans, trimmed
- 3 tablespoons unsalted butter
- 1 large red onion, quartered and thinly sliced
- 2 cloves garlic, peeled and minced
- 1 1/2 teaspoons red wine vinegar
- 3 tablespoons chicken broth
- salt and pepper to taste
- 3 tablespoons finely chopped cilantro

Direction

- Boil a big pot of lightly salted water. Put green beans in the water and cook for 3 minutes. Take off from heat, drain in a colander. Put under cold water until it's not hot. Drain then pat dry.

- In a medium skillet, melt 1 tbsp. butter on medium heat. Mix in garlic and onion. Sauté until onions are tender. Melt leftover butter in skillet. Mix green beans in. Mix in broth and vinegar. Season with pepper and salt. Stir in cilantro. Lower heat, simmer, covered, for 15 minutes or until the green beans are tender.

Nutrition Information

- Calories: 66 calories;
- Sodium: 7
- Total Carbohydrate: 8.2
- Cholesterol: 9
- Protein: 1.9
- Total Fat: 3.6

14. Greek Green Beans

Serving: 8 | Prep: 20mins | Ready in:

Ingredients

- 3/4 cup olive oil
- 2 cups chopped onions
- 1 clove garlic, minced
- 2 pounds fresh green beans, rinsed and trimmed
- 3 large tomatoes, diced
- 2 teaspoons sugar
- salt to taste

Direction

- In a big skillet, heat the olive oil over medium heat. Cook and mix in the garlic and onions in the skillet until they become tender.
- IStir the salt, sugar, tomatoes and green beans into the skillet. Turn heat down to low then keep on cooking until beans become soft, another 45 minutes.

Nutrition Information

- Calories: 243 calories;
- Protein: 3
- Total Fat: 20.6
- Sodium: 12
- Total Carbohydrate: 14.6
- Cholesterol: 0

15. Green Bean Casserole By Kikkoman

Serving: 8 | Prep: | Ready in:

Ingredients

- 1 1/2 pounds fresh string beans, blanched
- 5 tablespoons butter or margarine
- 1 (10 ounce) package fresh mushrooms, sliced
- 1/2 cup sliced onions
- 2 cloves garlic, crushed
- 1 (10.75 ounce) can cream of mushroom soup
- 1 cup Kikkoman Panko Bread Crumbs

Direction

- Place blanched string beans in an oiled casserole dish's bottom, in a large skillet, melt butter. Sauté garlic, mushrooms and onion in melted butter until onions are tender. Pour in cream of mushroom soup. Mix until all the ingredients in the pan are combined; pour over the string beans. Scatter with Panko bread crumbs. Bake for 20 minutes at 350°F in the oven until breadcrumbs turned browned.

Nutrition Information

- Calories: 162 calories;
- Total Carbohydrate: 16.9
- Cholesterol: 19
- Protein: 3.6
- Total Fat: 9.9
- Sodium: 309

16. Green Bean Cheddar Casserole

Serving: 8 | Prep: | Ready in:

Ingredients

- 1 1/2 cups shredded Dietz Watson White NY C-Sharp Cheddar Cheese
- 1 (10.75 ounce) can cream of mushroom soup
- 1/2 cup milk
- 1 teaspoon soy sauce
- Dash ground black pepper
- 4 cups cooked cut green beans
- 1 1/3 cups French-fried onions

Direction

- In a 1 1/2-qt. casserole, mix the black pepper, beans, a 2/3 cup of onions, milk, soup, a cup of cheddar cheese, and soy sauce.
- Let it bake inside the 350°F oven for 25 minutes until the bean mixture is bubbling and heated through. Mix the bean mixture and sprinkle it with the remaining onions and cheddar cheese.
- Bake for 5 more minutes until the cheese and onions appear golden browned.

Nutrition Information

- Calories: 381 calories;
- Protein: 6.6
- Total Fat: 28.2
- Sodium: 746
- Total Carbohydrate: 23.3
- Cholesterol: 22

17. Green Bean Soup

Serving: 6 | Prep: 15mins | Ready in:

Ingredients

- 2 pounds fresh green beans
- 1 clove garlic, minced
- 1 sprig fresh parsley
- 1 pinch salt
- 2 slices bacon
- 3 tablespoons all-purpose flour
- 1 onion, chopped
- 1 cup sour cream
- 3 tablespoons vinegar

Direction

- Mix water to cover, salt, parsley, garlic, and green beans together over medium heat in a big pot and cook until the beans are soft.
- Fry bacon until crunchy, put aside. Add flour and onion to the bacon grease, mixing until brown and smooth. Pour in some water from the beans, whisking continually and slowly to avoid lumps.
- Cook until thickened a bit, and then add to the bean soup and boil. Mix vinegar, sour cream, and crisp bacon.

Nutrition Information

- Calories: 196 calories;
- Total Fat: 12.5
- Sodium: 111
- Total Carbohydrate: 17.6
- Cholesterol: 23
- Protein: 5.8

18. Green Bean And Potato Casserole

Serving: 6 | Prep: 15mins | Ready in:

Ingredients

- 2 (14 ounce) cans green beans, drained
- 2 (15 ounce) cans diced potatoes, drained
- 1 (10.75 ounce) can condensed cream of chicken soup

- 1 pound shredded Colby cheese

Direction

- Turn oven to 350°F (175°C) to preheat. Lightly oil a small casserole dish. In the prepared casserole dish, combine cheese, cream of chicken soup, potatoes, and green beans. Bake, covered in the preheated oven for half an hour. Uncover, and keep baking until casserole is lightly browned and bubbly, or for 15 minutes.

Nutrition Information

- Calories: 450 calories;
- Total Carbohydrate: 29
- Cholesterol: 76
- Protein: 22.3
- Total Fat: 27.5
- Sodium: 1467

19. Green Beans

Serving: 6 | Prep: 5mins | Ready in:

Ingredients

- 2 (14.5 ounce) cans green beans, drained
- 1/4 cup butter, melted
- 1/2 teaspoon garlic powder
- 1/2 cup brown sugar
- 1/2 pound bacon

Direction

- Preheat the oven to 190 degrees C (375 degrees F).
- Add the green beans into the baking dish. In a bowl, combine garlic powder, brown sugar and butter; add on top of the green beans. Arrange the bacon strips on top of beans.
- Bake in the preheated oven for roughly half an hour till green beans soften and bacon is cooked.

Nutrition Information

- Calories: 236 calories;
- Sodium: 699
- Total Carbohydrate: 24.3
- Cholesterol: 34
- Protein: 6.3
- Total Fat: 13

20. Green Beans With Orange Olive Oil

Serving: 4 | Prep: 15mins | Ready in:

Ingredients

- 3/4 pound fresh green beans, trimmed and halved
- 4 1/2 teaspoons extra-virgin olive oil
- 1 tablespoon orange zest strips
- kosher salt to taste
- 1 teaspoon grated orange zest

Direction

- In a steamer basket on top of an inch boiling water, put the green beans and cover. Let cook for 2 to 4 minutes till beans are soft yet remain firm. Drain; retain warmth.
- In the meantime, in a large skillet, mix together 1 tablespoon orange zest strips and olive oil over medium-low heat. Let cook and mix for about 2 minutes till olive oil has been infused with flavor of orange zest. Get rid of zest strips.
- With flavored olive oil and kosher salt, toss the drained green beans over medium heat till beans are covered in oil and hot. Put onto a serving platter and garnish with leftover 1 teaspoon grated orange zest.

Nutrition Information

- Calories: 76 calories;
- Cholesterol: 0
- Protein: 1.6
- Total Fat: 5.4
- Sodium: 105
- Total Carbohydrate: 6.6

21. Green Beans And Tofu

Serving: 4 | Prep: 10mins | Ready in:

Ingredients

- 1 (12 ounce) package firm tofu, cubed
- 5 tablespoons olive oil, divided
- 1/2 teaspoon chili powder, or to taste
- salt and freshly ground black pepper to taste
- 1 pound fresh green beans, trimmed
- 1 clove garlic, minced
- 1 teaspoon seasoned salt

Direction

- In a bowl, mix together pepper, salt, chili powder, 1/4 cup olive oil, and tofu and let marinate, about 10-20 minutes.
- Boil water in a pot; add beans and cook for 15-20 minutes until soft but not mushy. Strain.
- In a skillet, heat the leftover 1 tablespoon olive oil over medium heat. Put in tofu and cook for 3 minutes until turning light brown, tossing sometimes. Add garlic and cook for another 1 minute. Add beans and use seasoned salt, pepper, and salt to season.

Nutrition Information

- Calories: 252 calories;
- Total Fat: 21.1
- Sodium: 285
- Total Carbohydrate: 10.4
- Cholesterol: 0
- Protein: 9

22. Green Beans For A Special Occasion

Serving: 4 | Prep: 10mins | Ready in:

Ingredients

- 1 tablespoon olive oil
- 1 clove garlic, minced
- 1/4 cup chopped pine nuts
- 1 pound fresh green beans, trimmed and snapped
- salt and pepper to taste

Direction

- In a skillet, heat olive oil over medium heat. Mix in pine nuts and garlic then sauté until light brown.
- In a medium saucepan, put the green beans and enough water to cover the green beans. Boil. Use pepper and salt to season. Cook until beans become tender, about 5 minutes. Drain then toss with the pine nuts and garlic. Serve.

Nutrition Information

- Calories: 114 calories;
- Total Fat: 8
- Sodium: 292
- Total Carbohydrate: 9.3
- Cholesterol: 0
- Protein: 4

23. Green Beans With Almonds And Caramelized Shallots

Serving: 6 | Prep: 20mins | Ready in:

Ingredients

- 1/4 cup blanched slivered almonds
- 3 tablespoons butter
- 5 small shallots, thinly sliced
- 1 red bell pepper, chopped
- 2 tablespoons white sugar
- salt and pepper to taste
- 1 1/2 pounds fresh green beans, trimmed and snapped

Direction

- In a dry skillet, arrange the slivered almonds on low heat, stir frequently and cook for 3-5 minutes until the almonds get toasted lightly. Observe carefully to prevent them from burning. Take the almonds away and put aside.
- In a skillet, heat the butter on medium-low heat, stir and cook the red bell pepper and shallots for around 8 minutes until getting soft. Use pepper, salt, and sugar to dust over the shallot mixture, and turn down the heat to low. Slowly cook and occasionally stir, covered, for 5-8 minutes until the shallots caramelize and sugar dissolves.
- Arrange a steamer insert into a saucepan, pour in water to just below the steamer's bottom, and allow to boil the water. Add in the green beans, and steam, covered, for 7-8 minutes until just becoming tender enough to be fork-tender. Let drain the green beans, put them into the skillet with shallot mixture, combine properly, add in the toasted almonds and carefully stir.

Nutrition Information

- Calories: 148 calories;
- Total Fat: 8.3
- Sodium: 51
- Total Carbohydrate: 17.1
- Cholesterol: 15
- Protein: 3.7

24. Green Beans With Smokey Bacon Vinaigrette

Serving: 8 | Prep: 10mins | Ready in:

Ingredients

- 2 pounds fresh green beans, trimmed
- 1/2 pound smoked bacon, cut into 1/2-inch pieces
- 1 yellow onion, sliced thin
- 1/3 cup red wine vinegar
- 1 tablespoon white sugar
- 1/4 cup chopped fresh flat-leaf parsley

Direction

- Create the ice bath by filling a big pot with the water and ice; put aside.
- Boil a pot of slightly salted water. Cook green beans in boiling water for roughly 3 minutes or till turning soften slightly but crisp. Drain. Plunge immediately the green beans into ice bath to stop cooking process. Drain and put aside.
- Cook bacon on medium high heat in the big and deep skillet for roughly 5 minutes till it starts to brown. Put onions into bacon and keep cooking for 7-10 minutes till onions start to caramelizes and become golden brown. Put in sugar, red wine vinegar and green beans; cook and whisk for 2-3 minutes till sugar dissolves.

Nutrition Information

- Calories: 186 calories;
- Total Fat: 13
- Sodium: 245
- Total Carbohydrate: 13.3
- Cholesterol: 19
- Protein: 5.7

25. Ground Turkey And Red Potato Veggie Soup

Serving: 6 | Prep: 30mins | Ready in:

Ingredients

- 5 cups low-sodium chicken broth
- 3 cups water
- 1 cup chopped zucchini
- 1/2 cup frozen corn
- 3 carrots, sliced
- 3 red potatoes, cubed
- 2 stalks celery, diced
- 1/2 cup frozen peas
- 1/2 cup frozen green beans
- 1/4 cup olive oil
- 1 pound ground turkey
- 1/2 large yellow onion, diced
- 1 tablespoon minced garlic
- 1 tablespoon kosher salt
- 1/2 teaspoon ground cumin
- 1/2 teaspoon ground coriander
- 1/2 teaspoon ground turmeric
- 1 teaspoon tomato paste
- 2 bay leaves
- 1/2 cup uncooked white rice
- 1/2 bunch cilantro, chopped

Direction

- In a large pot, combine green beans, peas, celery, potatoes, carrots, corn, zucchini, water, and chicken broth, then boil. Decrease heat and simmer for 10 minutes until the vegetables are slightly soft.
- In a pan, heat oil on medium-high heat and add turkey, then cook, stirring, while breaking them into small pieces for 5 - 7 minutes until they are brown. Add garlic and onions, then season with turmeric, coriander, cumin, and 1/2 teaspoon salt. Pour the mixture into the vegetable mixture, then add bay leaves, tomato paste, and the remaining salt. Decrease the heat to low and simmer for 1 hour until the vegetables become soft.

Stir in rice and simmer for another 15 minutes until tender. Serve soup in bowls and topped with cilantro.

Nutrition Information

- Calories: 333 calories;
- Cholesterol: 59
- Protein: 21.4
- Total Fat: 15.6
- Sodium: 1165
- Total Carbohydrate: 28.1

corn, carrots, pepper, and salt. Stew over low heat for 30 minutes, until the soup is hot and the flavors are well blended.

Nutrition Information

- Calories: 268 calories;
- Total Fat: 6.9
- Sodium: 756
- Total Carbohydrate: 39.2
- Cholesterol: 27
- Protein: 13.3

26. Home Style Vegetable Beef Soup

Serving: 10 | Prep: 10mins | Ready in:

Ingredients

- 1 pound ground beef
- 1 onion, diced
- 6 red potatoes, finely diced
- 5 carrots, thinly sliced
- 1/2 cup water
- 1 (15 ounce) can whole kernel corn, drained
- 2 cups frozen green beans
- 1 (46 fluid ounce) bottle tomato-vegetable juice cocktail
- 1 cup water
- 1 teaspoon salt
- 1 teaspoon ground black pepper

Direction

- On medium heat, cook beef, potatoes, and onion in a large pot for 10-15 minutes, covered, until the potatoes are tender and beef is no longer pink.
- In the meantime, put 1/2 cup water and carrots in a microwave-safe bowl; microwave on high until softened, about 5 minutes.
- Let the beef mixture drain and put back to the pot with water, juice cocktail, green beans,

27. Italian Lamb Stew

Serving: 6 | Prep: 25mins | Ready in:

Ingredients

- 2 tablespoons olive oil
- 1 1/2 pounds boneless lamb shoulder, cut into 1-inch cubes
- salt and ground black pepper to taste
- 5 cloves garlic, sliced thin
- 1/2 cup red wine
- 1/2 cup chicken broth
- 4 cups peeled, chopped tomatoes
- 1 teaspoon dried oregano
- 1 bay leaf
- 4 potatoes, peeled and cut into 1-inch pieces
- 2 cups fresh green beans, trimmed
- 1 red bell pepper, seeded and cut into 1-inch pieces
- 2 small zucchini, sliced
- 3 tablespoons chopped fresh parsley

Direction

- In a Dutch oven or in a large heavy-bottom pot, heat olive oil. Sprinkle lamb with salt and pepper to season and cook in hot oil for 2 to 3 minutes until brown in color. Add garlic and cook, for 1 minute, remember to stir while cooking. Pour chicken broth and red wine into the pan; bring to a boil, remember to use a wooden spoon to scrape out all the browned bits in the bottom of the pot while boiling. Lower the heat to medium low; and add bay leaf, oregano and tomatoes to the pot. Bring to a gentle boil for about 45 minutes until the lamb is softened.

- Raise the heat to medium-high. Add zucchini, red pepper, green bean and potatoes to the pot. Cook for an additional 15 to 20 minutes until vegetables are softened. Scatter parsley over soup. Remove bay leaf and add salt and pepper to season. Serve.

Nutrition Information

- Calories: 389 calories;
- Total Carbohydrate: 38
- Cholesterol: 58
- Protein: 20.3
- Total Fat: 16.7
- Sodium: 283

28. Jamie's Minestrone

Serving: 8 | Prep: 35mins | Ready in:

Ingredients

- 3 tablespoons olive oil
- 3 cloves garlic, chopped
- 2 onions, chopped
- 2 cups chopped celery
- 5 carrots, sliced
- 2 cups chicken broth
- 2 cups water
- 4 cups tomato sauce
- 1/2 cup red wine (optional)
- 1 cup canned kidney beans, drained
- 1 (15 ounce) can green beans
- 2 cups baby spinach, rinsed
- 3 zucchinis, quartered and sliced
- 1 tablespoon chopped fresh oregano
- 2 tablespoons chopped fresh basil

- salt and pepper to taste
- 1/2 cup seashell pasta
- 2 tablespoons grated Parmesan cheese for topping
- 1 tablespoon olive oil

Direction

- Heat the olive oil in a big stock pot over moderately-low heat and sauté the garlic for 2 to 3 minutes. Put in the onion and sauté for 4 to 5 minutes. Put in the carrots and celery, sauté for 1 to 2 minutes.
- Put in the tomato sauce, water and chicken broth; boil, mixing often. If wished put red wine at this stage. Turn the heat down to low and put in pepper, salt, basil, oregano, zucchini, spinach leaves, green beans and kidney beans. Simmer for 30 to 40 minutes, the longer the better.
- Pour water in a medium saucepan and boil. Put in the macaroni and cook till soft. Drain the water and reserve.
- In separate serving bowls, put 2 tablespoons of cooked pasta when soup is heated through and pasta is cooked. Scoop the soup over pasta and scatter Parmesan cheese over top. Sprinkle with olive oil, serve.

Nutrition Information

- Calories: 227 calories;
- Total Fat: 8.3
- Sodium: 1142
- Total Carbohydrate: 30
- Cholesterol: 1
- Protein: 8.6

29. Marilyn's Green Beans Italiano

Serving: 6 | Prep: 20mins | Ready in:

Ingredients

- 1 1/2 pounds fresh green beans, trimmed and cut into 1-inch pieces
- 1/4 cup butter
- 1/2 cup Italian-seasoned bread crumbs
- 1/4 cup grated Parmesan cheese
- salt and pepper to taste
- 1 1/2 teaspoons chopped fresh parsley

Direction

- Put the green beans with enough water to cover in a saucepan with a lid. Boil. Lower to low heat, let simmer while covered for about 10 minutes, until the beans get tender but crisp. Drain. Arrange the beans on paper towels to dry.
- Add butter to a big frying pan and melt it over moderate-low heat, mix in Parmesan cheese and the breadcrumbs. Lower to low heat, add the beans; stir and cook for about 3 minutes, until the crumbs start to brown and the beans are heated through. Add pepper and salt for seasoning. Dredge with the parsley and serve.

Nutrition Information

- Calories: 156 calories;
- Total Fat: 9.5
- Sodium: 283
- Total Carbohydrate: 14.9
- Cholesterol: 23
- Protein: 4.7

30. Mediterranean Rice Salad

Serving: 6 | Prep: 15mins | Ready in:

Ingredients

- 3 tablespoons extra-virgin olive oil, divided
- 1 cup uncooked long grain white rice
- 2 1/2 cups water
- 1 cup drained canned French style green beans
- 1 cup pitted black olives

- 1 roasted red pepper, drained and diced
- 1 green bell pepper, diced
- 1 dill pickle spear, diced
- 2 roma (plum) tomatoes, diced
- 3 cloves garlic, finely chopped
- 1 tablespoon white wine vinegar

Direction

- Heat 2 tbsp. of the olive oil on medium heat in a skillet. Whisk in the rice, and cook till slightly brown. Add water. Boil, lower the heat to low and let it simmer till all of the liquid is absorbed.
- In a big bowl, combine garlic, tomatoes, pickle, green pepper, red pepper, olives and green beans. Toss with rice. Drizzle with the rest 1 tbsp. of the olive oil and vinegar, and coat by tossing. Keep covered, and keep in the refrigerator till becoming cool totally or for 60 minutes, prior to serving.

Nutrition Information

- Calories: 229 calories;
- Total Fat: 9.7
- Sodium: 607
- Total Carbohydrate: 31.9
- Cholesterol: 0
- Protein: 3.6

31. Monica's Vegetable And Seitan Stew

Serving: 4 | Prep: 15mins | Ready in:

Ingredients

- 1 cup uncooked brown rice
- 2 1/2 cups water
- 1 quart vegetable broth
- 1 (14.5 ounce) can diced tomatoes with garlic
- 1 (8 ounce) package seitan
- 1 cup cauliflower

- 2 carrots, chopped
- 1/2 cup chopped fresh green beans
- 1/4 cup sliced green onions
- celery salt to taste

Direction

- Bring the rice and water in a pot to a boil. Lower the heat to low, and simmer, covered for 45 minutes.
- Bring the broth in a separate pot to a boil. Stir in the seitan, tomatoes, carrots, green onions, green beans, and cauliflower. Decrease to low heat, and simmer for 10 minutes or until vegetables are tender. Add celery salt to season, and serve on top of cooked rice in bowls.

Nutrition Information

- Calories: 300 calories;
- Sodium: 1231
- Total Carbohydrate: 50.1
- Cholesterol: 0
- Protein: 19.4
- Total Fat: 3.4

32. Moody's Green Beans

Serving: 5 | Prep: 10mins | Ready in:

Ingredients

- 1 pound pork sausage
- 1 (10.75 ounce) can condensed cream of mushroom soup
- 2 (14.5 ounce) cans green beans, drained

Direction

- Crumble sausage in a medium skillet and fry on moderately high heat until brown, then drain the grease. Set the oven to 175°C or 350°F to preheat.

- Combine together green beans, mushroom soup and sausage in an 8-inch x8-inch casserole dish. Blend in 1 cup of sour cream if wanted. Use foil to cover the dish and bake for half an hour. Use 1 cup of shredded cheese to sprinkle over top if you want and turn back to the oven to bake for 5 minutes longer without a cover, until cheese melts.

Nutrition Information

- Calories: 390 calories;
- Sodium: 1613
- Total Carbohydrate: 10.4
- Cholesterol: 70
- Protein: 17.1
- Total Fat: 31.3

33. Okonomiyaki

Serving: 6 | Prep: 12mins | Ready in:

Ingredients

- 1 cup chopped cooked chicken
- 1 1/2 cups thinly sliced napa cabbage
- 1/4 cup shredded carrots
- 3 green onions, chopped
- 12 fresh green beans, cut into 1/2 inch pieces
- 1 small green bell pepper, cut into thin strips
- 1 small zucchini, cut into thin strips
- 3 eggs, lightly beaten
- 3/4 cup all-purpose flour
- 3/4 cup chicken stock
- 2 teaspoons soy sauce
- 1 teaspoon vegetable oil
- 1/4 teaspoon toasted sesame oil

Direction

- Mix zucchini, chicken, green bell pepper, cabbage, green beans, green onions, and carrots in a big bowl. Whisk soy sauce, eggs, chicken stock, and flour together in another bowl; toss into the chicken mixture to coat well.

- On medium heat, stir sesame oil and vegetable oil in a pan. Spoon a quarter cup of batter in the pan just enough to form a 2 1/2-in. round; cover. Cook for 4 mins, or until golden brown on the bottom. Turn then keep cooking for 4 mins, or until completely cooked. Place on paper towels to drain.

Nutrition Information

- Calories: 156 calories;
- Sodium: 279
- Total Carbohydrate: 16.1
- Cholesterol: 112
- Protein: 12.7
- Total Fat: 4.5

34. Pastelon (Puerto Rican Layered Casserole)

Serving: 8 | Prep: 25mins | Ready in:

Ingredients

- 1 pound lean ground beef
- 1 cup tomato sauce
- 1/3 cup sofrito
- 8 green olives, finely chopped
- 1 teaspoon crushed garlic
- 1 teaspoon salt, divided
- 1/4 cup recao
- 1/4 teaspoon dried oregano
- cooking spray
- 3/4 cup vegetable oil
- 6 large ripe plantains - peeled, halved, and each half cut lengthwise into 4 slices
- 5 large eggs
- 1 (9 ounce) package frozen French cut green beans, thawed and drained
- 1 cup shredded mozzarella cheese

Direction

- At medium heat, place a big skillet on top to heat it. Insert the ground beef, cooking and stirring for around 10 minutes until it is not pink and the exterior is brown. Move the meat out of the pan then drain the fat. Insert oregano, recao, 1/2 teaspoon of salt, garlic, green olives, sofrito and tomato sauce into skillet, cooking and stirring for 5 minutes at medium to low heat. Move the ground beef back into the skillet and lower the heat until it's simmering. Without the cover on, continue cooking for another 15 minutes. During the process, stir from time to time. Preheat the oven to 350°F/175°C. Use cooking spray to layer a baking pan (8 by 8 inches). In a big skillet, add the oil at medium to high heat to 350°F/175°C. Insert the slices of plantain, frying for 3-5 minutes on each side until both sides are golden. Move them onto paper towels to be drained. In a bowl, whisk the eggs together until combined. Insert 1/2 teaspoon of salt. Use 1/2 the plantains to line the baking pan's base. If necessary, let them overlap. Place the rest of the green beans, ground beef mixture and the rest of the plantains atop. Finish by pouring the eggs atop. Put the mozzarella cheese on everything else. Put it into the preheated oven, baking for 20-25 minutes until the cheese melts and the eggs start setting.

Nutrition Information

- Calories: 463 calories;
- Sodium: 678
- Total Carbohydrate: 70.2
- Cholesterol: 149
- Protein: 18.3
- Total Fat: 15.2

35. Pickled Green Beans

Serving: 8 | Prep: 10mins | Ready in:

Ingredients

- 2 pounds fresh green beans, rinsed and trimmed
- 4 cloves garlic, peeled
- 8 sprigs fresh dill weed
- 4 teaspoons salt
- 2 1/2 cups white vinegar
- 2 1/2 cups water

Direction

- Cut green beans to fit inside pint canning jars.
- Put in a steamer set over 1 in. of boiling water with green beans and cover. Cook about 3 minutes, until softened but still firm.
- Pack into 4 hot and sterilized pint jars with the beans. Put into each jar against the glass with 2 sprigs dill weed and 1 clove garlic. Add to each jar with 1 tsp. salt.
- Bring vinegar and water in a big saucepan to a boil on high heat, then drizzle over beans.
- Fit the jars with rings and lids and process in a boiling water bath about 10 minutes.

Nutrition Information

- Calories: 39 calories;
- Total Fat: 0.1
- Sodium: 1170
- Total Carbohydrate: 8.6
- Cholesterol: 0
- Protein: 2.2

36. Poor Man's Pie

Serving: 8 | Prep: 10mins | Ready in:

Ingredients

- 1 pound ground beef
- salt and ground black pepper to taste
- 1 pinch garlic powder, or to taste
- 1 pinch onion powder, or to taste
- 1 (10.75 ounce) can cream of mushroom soup

- 2 (15 ounce) cans green beans, drained
- 5 cups mashed potatoes
- 2 cups shredded Cheddar cheese

Direction

- Set an oven to 175°C (350°F) and start preheating.
- In a large skillet, stir and cook the ground beef over medium heat for 10 minutes until it is crumbly and browned; flavor with onion powder, garlic powder, black pepper, and salt. Drain off excess oil. Stir green beans and cream of mushroom soup into the ground beef, then bring to a simmer.
- Arrange the ground beef mixture in a 9x13-inch casserole dish. Distribute the mashed potatoes onto the ground beef mixture evenly. Dust the top with Cheddar cheese.
- In the prepared oven, bake for 20 minutes until heated through.

Nutrition Information

- Calories: 372 calories;
- Total Fat: 19.1
- Sodium: 1022
- Total Carbohydrate: 29
- Cholesterol: 67
- Protein: 20.5

37. Quick And Fast Vegetarian Vegetable Soup In A Hurry

Serving: 6 | Prep: 15mins | Ready in:

Ingredients

- 2 tablespoons coconut oil
- 1 onion, chopped
- 2 garlic cloves, minced
- 4 cups low-sodium vegetable broth
- 1 (15 ounce) can tomato sauce
- 1 (24 ounce) bag frozen stew vegetables

- 1 cup frozen corn
- 1 cup frozen green beans
- 1 teaspoon ground black pepper
- salt to taste

Direction

- Place a large pot on medium heat, heat coconut oil. Put in garlic and onion; cook while stirring for 4-5 minutes till onion is translucent. Add tomato sauce and vegetable broth; allow to simmer for around 5 minutes. Mix in green beans, corn and stew vegetables; simmer for 15-20 minutes till tender. Taste with salt and black pepper.

Nutrition Information

- Calories: 190 calories;
- Total Fat: 5.5
- Sodium: 583
- Total Carbohydrate: 33.4
- Cholesterol: 0
- Protein: 6.3

38. Red Winter Minestrone With Winter Greens Pesto

Serving: 4 | Prep: 20mins | Ready in:

Ingredients

- Winter Greens Pesto:
- 1 bunch beet greens
- 1 bunch turnip greens
- 1 bunch kale
- 2/3 cup extra-virgin olive oil
- 2 cloves garlic
- 1 ounce Parmigiano Reggiano cheese, grated
- 1/2 teaspoon kosher salt
- Red Winter Minestrone:
- 6 tablespoons extra-virgin olive oil, divided
- 1 white onion, finely chopped
- 2 Roma (plum) tomatoes, peeled and grated

- 4 cloves garlic, minced
- 1 teaspoon minced fresh rosemary
- 1/2 teaspoon kosher salt
- 1 bay leaf
- 1 pinch dried chili flakes
- 1 leek, white and light green parts only, halved lengthwise, cleaned, and cut into 1/2-inch slices
- 1 carrot, peeled and sliced
- 1/2 pound turnips, peeled and cubed
- 1/2 pound beets, peeled and cubed
- 1 cup dry white wine
- 2 cups cooked cannellini beans
- 1/2 cup green beans, cut into 1-inch pieces
- 5 cups water
- 1/4 cup chopped flat-leaf (Italian) parsley
- 1/2 tablespoon fresh lemon juice, or to taste (optional)

Direction

- Boil big pot with salted water; prep bowl with ice water. Strip kale, turnip greens and beet greens from coarse stems; wash leaves well. In batches, cook every bunch in boiling water for about 1 minute till slightly limp and bright green. Immediately transfer to ice water; repeat with leftover greens. Throw cooking water.
- Take greens from ice water; squeeze as much water out as you can.
- Blend 1/2 tsp. kosher salt, Parmigiano Reggiano cheese, 2 garlic cloves, 2/3 cup olive oil and greens till smooth in food processor/blender. Put pesto in bowl; use plastic wrap to cover surface.
- In big pot, heat 1/4 cup olive oil on medium high heat; mix chili flakes, bay leaf, 1/2 tsp. kosher salt, rosemary, 4 minced garlic cloves, grated tomato and onion in. Cook for 5 minutes, frequently mixing; lower heat to low. Mix and cook for 20-30 minutes till veggies are deep golden brown.
- Put leftover 2 tbsp. olive oil on onion mixture; mix beets, turnips, carrot and leek in. Put heat on medium high; cook for 5 minutes, occasionally mixing.

- Put white wine on veggie mixture; scrape off browned bits from bottom of pot. Mix green beans and cannellini beans into veggie mixture; put 5 cups water in. Boil liquid; lower heat. Simmer for about 5 more minutes till green beans are tender. Mix lemon juice and parsley in.
- Divide soup to heated bowls; serve with generous dollop of winter greens pesto.

Nutrition Information

- Calories: 916 calories;
- Sodium: 808
- Total Carbohydrate: 65.7
- Cholesterol: 6
- Protein: 20.4
- Total Fat: 61.4

39. Sesame Tempura Green Beans

Serving: 4 | Prep: 10mins | Ready in:

Ingredients

- 2 quarts oil for deep frying
- 1 cup all-purpose flour
- 1/4 cup sesame seeds
- 1 (12 fluid ounce) can or bottle beer
- 3/4 pound fresh green beans, rinsed and trimmed
- salt to taste
- 3 tablespoons soy sauce
- 3 teaspoons lime juice
- 1 teaspoon white sugar

Direction

- Place a deep-fryer on 375°F (190°C); heat oil.
- Combine beer, sesame seeds and flour together in a medium bowl till smooth. Coat the beans with the flour mixture.

- Fry small batches of the coated beans for 1 1/2 minutes each batch, till golden brown. Strain on paper towels. Season with salt.
- Blend sugar, lime juice and soy sauce together in a small bowl; use as dipping sauce.

Nutrition Information

- Calories: 630 calories;
- Sodium: 687
- Total Carbohydrate: 37.5
- Cholesterol: 0
- Protein: 7.6
- Total Fat: 48.9

40. Shrimp Scampi Over Rice From Knorr®

Serving: 4 | Prep: 10mins | Ready in:

Ingredients

- 2 tablespoons I Can't Believe It's Not Butter!® Spread, divided
- 1 pound uncooked large shrimp
- 2 cloves garlic, finely chopped
- 2 tablespoons lemon juice
- 1 (5.4 ounce) package Knorr® Rice Sides™ - Herb Butter, prepared according to package directions
- 1 (10 ounce) package frozen cut green beans, prepared according to package directions

Direction

- If necessary, use pepper and salt to season shrimp. Melt one tablespoon Spread in a 12-inch nonstick skillet on the medium high heat and cook shrimp for 3 minutes till shrimp becomes pink while mixing once in a while.
- Mix in garlic and cook for half a minute. Take the skillet out of heat and mix in leftover 1 tbsp. of Spread and lemon juice till melted the Spread.

- Mix into hot Knorr Rice Sides – Herb Butter alongside green beans.

Nutrition Information

- Calories: 299 calories;
- Sodium: 265
- Total Carbohydrate: 14.7
- Cholesterol: 174
- Protein: 23.1
- Total Fat: 8.6

41. Sinigang Na Baka

Serving: 6 | Prep: 15mins | Ready in:

Ingredients

- 2 tablespoons canola oil
- 1 large onion, chopped
- 2 cloves garlic, chopped
- 1 pound beef stew meat, cut into 1 inch cubes
- 1 quart water
- 2 large tomatoes, diced
- 1/2 pound fresh green beans, rinsed and trimmed
- 1/2 medium head bok choy, cut into 1 1/2 inch strips
- 1 head fresh broccoli, cut into bite size pieces
- 1 (1.41 ounce) package tamarind soup base

Direction

- In a medium stock pot, add oil. Stir-fry garlic and onion until tender. Put the beef to the pot, and stir-fry until browned. Add in water. Make it boil, lower heat, and boil for 20-30 minutes.
- Add green beans and tomatoes into the pot, and keep on simmering for 10 minutes. Mix in tamarind soup mix, broccoli, and bok choy. Simmer for 10 more minutes.

Nutrition Information

- Calories: 304 calories;
- Total Fat: 19.7
- Sodium: 1405
- Total Carbohydrate: 15
- Cholesterol: 51
- Protein: 17.8

42. Slow Cooker Green Beans, Ham And Potatoes

Serving: 10 | Prep: 30mins | Ready in:

Ingredients

- 2 pounds fresh green beans, rinsed and trimmed
- 1 large onion, chopped
- 3 ham hocks
- 1 1/2 pounds new potatoes, quartered
- 1 teaspoon garlic powder
- 1 teaspoon onion powder
- 1 teaspoon seasoning salt
- 1 tablespoon chicken bouillon granules
- ground black pepper to taste

Direction

- If beans are big, cut in half, add into the slow cooker along with water to barely cover, and put in the ham hocks and onion. Covered, and cook over High heat till simmering. Lower the heat to Low, and cook till the beans turn crispy but not done or for 2 - 3 hours.
- Put in the potatoes, and cook for 45 more minutes. When the potatoes are cooking, take the ham hocks out of the slow cooker, and debone the meat. Cut or shred the meat, and bring back into the slow cooker. Use the pepper, bouillon, seasoning salt, onion powder and garlic powder to season. Cook till the potatoes are done, then adjust the seasoning to your taste.

- To serve, with the slotted spoon, add the ham, potatoes and beans into a serving dish along with a little amount of the broth.

Nutrition Information

- Calories: 200 calories;
- Total Fat: 9
- Sodium: 133
- Total Carbohydrate: 20.6
- Cholesterol: 29
- Protein: 10.2

43. Smothered Green Beans

Serving: 6 | Prep: 20mins | Ready in:

Ingredients

- 6 thick slices bacon, chopped
- 1/2 cup onions, minced
- 1 teaspoon minced garlic
- 1 pound fresh green beans, trimmed
- 1 cup water
- 1/8 teaspoon salt
- 1 pinch ground black pepper

Direction

- Add the bacon into the big and deep skillet. Cook on medium-high heat till fat starts to render. Whisk in the garlic and onions; allow it to cook for 60 seconds. Whisk in the water and beans. Allow beans to cook till beans soften and water is evaporated. If beans are not soft when the water is evaporated, pour in a small amount of additional water and allow them to cook till soft. Use pepper and salt to season to taste and serve.

Nutrition Information

- Calories: 97 calories;
- Total Fat: 5.4

- Sodium: 343
- Total Carbohydrate: 7
- Cholesterol: 14
- Protein: 6.2

44. Southern Style Thanksgiving Green Beans

Serving: 8 | Prep: 40mins | Ready in:

Ingredients

- 2 quarts water
- 4 pounds fresh green beans, trimmed and snapped into 1 1/2 inch pieces
- 1 ham hock
- 1 onion, chopped
- 2 cloves garlic, finely chopped
- 1/4 cup distilled white vinegar
- 1 tablespoon salt
- 1/2 tablespoon black pepper

Direction

- In a big pot, add water, then mix in vinegar, garlic, onion, ham hock and green beans. Season with pepper and salt, then bring the mixture to a boil and cook for 10 minutes.
- Lower the heat to low and simmer for 4 hours. Take out the ham hock and cut the meat into small pieces, then take the meat back to the beans and serve.

Nutrition Information

- Calories: 144 calories;
- Total Fat: 5.6
- Sodium: 907
- Total Carbohydrate: 18
- Cholesterol: 17
- Protein: 8.6

45. Swiss Cheese Green Bean Casserole

Serving: 8 | Prep: 20mins | Ready in:

Ingredients

- 1 1/2 pounds fresh green beans, trimmed and snapped
- 2 tablespoons butter, melted
- 2 tablespoons all-purpose flour
- 2 tablespoons grated onion
- 1 teaspoon white sugar
- 1 teaspoon salt
- 2 cups sour cream
- 8 ounces coarsely shredded Swiss cheese
- 2 cups corn flakes, crushed
- 2 tablespoons butter, melted

Direction

- Set the oven to 400°F or 200°C for preheating.
- Position the steamer insert into the saucepan. Fill the pan with water to just beneath the bottom of the steamer. Boil the water, and then add the green beans. Cover up and steam the beans for 5 minutes, or until slightly tender.
- Mix together the sugar, flour, 2 tbsp. of butter, onion, and salt in a saucepan set over medium heat. Mix in sour cream gradually. Cook and stir for 10 minutes, or until the mixture is smooth, hot, and thick. Add the steamed green beans. Put the bean-cream mixture into a 2-qt casserole dish. Sprinkle the mixture with Swiss cheese.
- In a bowl, combine the 2 tbsp. of butter and corn flakes until evenly coated. Sprinkle the mixture all over the Swiss cheese layer.
- Let it bake inside the preheated oven for 20 minutes, or until the topping is browned and the cheese is bubbling.

Nutrition Information

- Calories: 343 calories;
- Total Fat: 25.9
- Sodium: 472

- Total Carbohydrate: 18.4
- Cholesterol: 67
- Protein: 11.8

46. Tater Tot Casserole IV

Serving: 6 | Prep: 15mins | Ready in:

Ingredients

- 1 pound lean ground beef
- 1 pound fresh, ground pork sausage
- 1 small onion, chopped
- 1 (10.75 ounce) can condensed cream of mushroom soup
- 1 (14.5 ounce) can French-style green beans, drained
- 1 (32 ounce) package tater tots, thawed
- salt to taste

Direction

- In a large skillet, sauté the onion until it is soft; put in sausage and beef, cook until they are brown. Drain and then put aside.
- Set an oven to 175°C (350°F) and start heating.
- Scatter beans and soup on the bottom of a 9x13 inch baking dish. Pour in the meat mixture slowly, then put tater tots on top and flavor to taste with salt.
- Bake at 175°C (350°F) until the casserole is fully cook, for 30-45 minutes.

Nutrition Information

- Calories: 725 calories;
- Total Carbohydrate: 44.8
- Cholesterol: 104
- Protein: 30.6
- Total Fat: 50.7
- Sodium: 1831

47. Tuna Nicoise Salad With Dijon Vinaigrette

Serving: 4 | Prep: 20mins | Ready in:

Ingredients

- Dressing:
- 2 tablespoons Dijon mustard
- 1/3 cup red wine vinegar
- 1 tablespoon chopped fresh parsley
- 1 teaspoon sugar
- 1/2 cup extra-virgin olive oil
- Salt and ground black pepper to taste
- Salad:
- 1 (14.5 ounce) can whole potatoes, drained and halved
- 1 (14.5 ounce) can French-style no salt added green beans, drained
- 1 (14 ounce) can artichoke hearts, well drained and quartered
- 1 (14 ounce) can sliced hearts of palm, drained
- 1 (5 ounce) can tuna packed in water, drained and gently flaked
- 1 (2.2 ounce) can sliced black olives, drained
- 1 large tomato, cut into wedges
- 2 hard-cooked eggs, cut into wedges

Direction

- To Prepare Dressing: Mix sugar, parsley, red wine vinegar, and mustard in a small bowl; slowly mix in olive oil till blended well. Add pepper and salt to taste.
- To Prepare Salad: Arrange hard-cooked eggs, tomato wedges, olives, tuna, hearts of palm, artichoke hearts, green beans, and potatoes on a big platter. Sprinkle salad with dressing.

Nutrition Information

- Calories: 494 calories;
- Total Fat: 33.4
- Sodium: 1758
- Total Carbohydrate: 31.8
- Cholesterol: 115
- Protein: 18.5

48. Turkey Potato Casserole

Serving: 6 | Prep: 30mins | Ready in:

Ingredients

- 1 pound cooked turkey meat, shredded
- 1 onion, chopped
- 1 (14.5 ounce) can green beans, drained
- 1 (10.75 ounce) can condensed cream of mushroom soup
- 8 ounces cubed Cheddar cheese
- 8 ounces shredded Cheddar cheese
- 4 cups prepared mashed potatoes

Direction

- Set an oven to 175°C (350°F) and start preheating.
- Layer the turkey into the bottom of a 9x13-inch baking dish. Layer onion and green beans on top so the turkey can't be seen. Spread the condensed soup onto the onion layer, then dust the shredded cheese on top. Mix mashed potatoes and cubed cheese together and spread on top of the casserole to cover.
- In the prepared oven, bake until heated through, about 30-40 minutes.

Nutrition Information

- Calories: 611 calories;
- Total Carbohydrate: 32.9
- Cholesterol: 140
- Protein: 45.3
- Total Fat: 32.6
- Sodium: 1466

49. Vegetable Cutlets

Serving: 6 | Prep: 15mins | Ready in:

Ingredients

- 2 large potatoes, peeled and diced
- 1 carrot, peeled and diced
- 1/2 cup fresh green beans, trimmed and snapped
- 1/4 cup frozen green peas
- 1 egg
- 1 1/2 cups bread crumbs
- 1/2 teaspoon garam masala
- 1/4 teaspoon cayenne pepper
- salt to taste
- 1/4 cup vegetable oil for frying

Direction

- In a saucepan, put peas, green beans, carrot and potatoes. Cover with enough water. Allow to boil; turn the heat down to low; simmer with a cover till the potatoes become tender, around 15 minutes. Strain vegetables, place into a bowl; use a potato masher to mash; keep a few small chunks.
- In the bowl with mashed vegetables, combine salt, cayenne pepper, garam masala, 3/4 cup of bread crumbs and egg together. Shape into 1/2-inch-thick patties. Coat with the remaining bread crumbs.
- Place a large frying pan on medium heat; heat oil. Fry in the coated patties till golden brown. Strain on paper towels.

Nutrition Information

- Calories: 234 calories;
- Total Fat: 3.4
- Sodium: 232
- Total Carbohydrate: 43.6
- Cholesterol: 31
- Protein: 7.7

50. Veggie Pot Pie

Serving: 6 | Prep: 30mins | Ready in:

Ingredients

- 2 tablespoons olive oil
- 1 onion, chopped
- 8 ounces mushrooms
- 1 clove garlic, minced
- 2 large carrots, diced
- 2 potatoes, peeled and diced
- 2 stalks celery, sliced 1/4 inch wide
- 2 cups cauliflower florets
- 1 cup fresh green beans, trimmed and snapped into 1/2 inch pieces
- 3 cups vegetable broth
- 1 teaspoon kosher salt
- 1 teaspoon ground black pepper
- 2 tablespoons cornstarch
- 2 tablespoons soy sauce
- 1 recipe pastry for double-crust pie

Direction

- Set an oven to preheat to 220°C (425°F).
- Heat the oil in a saucepan or a big skillet. Cook the garlic, mushrooms and onions in oil for 3-5 minutes, mixing often. Stir in celery, potatoes and carrots. Stir in vegetable broth, green beans and cauliflower, then boil. Lower the heat down to a simmer. Let it cook for about 5 minutes until the vegetables become barely tender. Sprinkle pepper and salt to season.
- Combine 1/4 cup of water, soy sauce and cornstarch in a small bowl, until the cornstarch becomes fully dissolved. Mix into the vegetables and let it cook for about 3 minutes until the sauce becomes thick.
- Roll out half of the dough to line an 11x7-inch baking dish. Pour the filling into the dish lined with pastry. Roll out the leftover dough, lay out on top the filling, then seal and flute the edges.
- Let it bake for 30 minutes in the preheated oven or until the crust turns brown.

Nutrition Information

- Calories: 469 calories;
- Sodium: 1198

- Total Carbohydrate: 54.4
- Cholesterol: 0
- Protein: 8.4
- Total Fat: 25

Index

Conclusion

Thank you again for downloading this book!

I hope you enjoyed reading about my book!

If you enjoyed this book, please take the time to share your thoughts and post a review on Amazon. It'd be greatly appreciated!

Write me an honest review about the book – I truly value your opinion and thoughts and I will incorporate them into my next book, which is already underway.

Thank you!

If you have any questions, **feel free to contact at:** *author@rutabagarecipes.com*

Pauline Harmon

rutabagarecipes.com

Printed in Great Britain
by Amazon